W9-DGG-568

JOE MONTANA
and the
San Francisco 49ers

SUPER BOWL XXIV

by Michael Sandler

Consultant: Norries Wilson
Head Football Coach
Columbia University

BEARPORT
PUBLISHING

New York, New York

Credits

Cover and Title Page, © George Rose/Getty Images; 4, © Rick Stewart/Allsport/
Getty Images; 5, © Zuma Press/Newscom.com; 6, Courtesy of Elinor Johnson;
7, Courtesy of Elinor Johnson; 8, © Tony Tomsic/WireImage/Getty Images; 9, ©
Walter Iooss Jr./Sports Illustrated; 11, © Richard Mackson/Sports Illustrated; 12,
© Bettmann/Corbis; 13, © Walter Iooss Jr./Sports Illustrated; 14, © Otto Greule
Jr/Getty Images; 15, © Arthur Anderson/WireImage/Getty Images; 16, © Wally
McNamee/Corbis; 17, © Ronald C. Modra/Sports Imagery/Getty Images; 18, © AP
Images/Rusty Kennedy; 19, © AP Images/Mark Duncan; 20, © Al Messerschmidt/
NFL/Getty Images; 21, © AP Images/Lennox McLennon; 22L, © Greg Trott/NFL/
Getty Images; 22R, © Otto Greule Jr/Getty Images.

Publisher: Kenn Goin
Senior Editor: Lisa Wiseman
Creative Director: Spencer Brinker
Design: Deborah Kaiser
Photo Researcher: James O'Connor

Library of Congress Cataloging-in-Publication Data

Sandler, Michael, 1965-
 Joe Montana and the San Francisco 49ers : Super Bowl XXIV / by Michael Sandler ;
consultant: Norries Wilson.
      p. cm. — (Super bowl superstars)
 Includes bibliographical references and index.
 ISBN-13: 978-1-59716-738-3 (library binding)
 ISBN-10: 1-59716-738-X (library binding)
 1. Montana, Joe, 1956—Juvenile literature. 2. Football players—United States—
Biography—Juvenile literature. 3. San Francisco 49ers (Football team) —Juvenile
literature. 4. Super Bowl (24th : 1990 : New Orleans, La.) —Juvenile literature. I.
Wilson, Norries. II. Title.

 GV939.M59S26 2009
 796.332092—dc22
 (B)
                              2008007017

For more information, write to Bearport Publishing Company, Inc., 101 Fifth Avenue,
Suite 6R, New York, New York 10003. Printed in the United States of America.

10 9 8 7 6 5 4 3 2 1

★ Contents ★

Another Win?

Over and over, Joe Montana stepped back into the **pocket**. The San Francisco 49ers' quarterback looked past the Denver Broncos' **defenders**. He scanned the field. He found his **receivers** and sent the ball flying.

Joe's passes were perfect **spirals** spinning toward their targets. As each one was caught, 49ers fans at Super Bowl XXIV (24) stood up and cheered.

Even for Joe—perhaps the greatest quarterback ever—this performance was amazing. Could he keep it up and bring his team another title?

Joe Montana

Joe (#16) looks to throw the ball to one of his receivers during Super Bowl XXIV (24) on January 28, 1990.

Joe had already led the 49ers to wins in Super Bowls XVI (16), XIX (19), and XXIII (23). Another win would tie the record for most victories by a team.

Born to Be a Quarterback

Joe Montana grew up about 25 miles (40 km) south of Pittsburgh, Pennsylvania. This area is known as football country. Like most of his neighbors, Joe learned to love football as a kid.

What Joe enjoyed most was throwing the ball. He practiced for hours by aiming the ball at an old car tire swinging from a tree.

It was no surprise that Joe became a star passer in high school. As his coach once said, Joe "was born to be a quarterback."

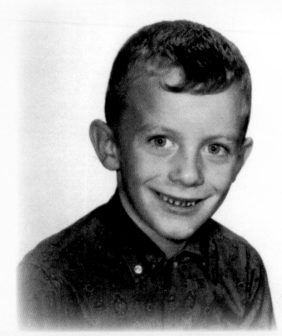

Joe grew up in Monongahela, Pennsylvania.

In his senior year of high school, Joe was named an **All-American**.

Comeback Kid

In college, Joe played for Notre Dame. He became famous for last-minute comebacks. When his team fell behind, Joe came into the game and brought them back to win.

Joe's arm wasn't the strongest, but he made up for it with his brain. Somehow, Joe knew what to do in every situation.

His control was excellent, too. His short, crisp passes always found their way to the right place.

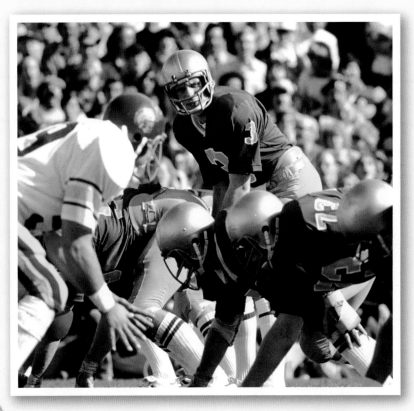

Joe (#3) lines up with the Notre Dame team, the Fighting Irish.

Joe playing for the Fighting Irish in a game against the University of Southern California

In 1978, Joe's Fighting Irish beat the Texas Longhorns, 38-10, in the **Cotton Bowl**. The win gave Notre Dame a national championship.

A Special Choice

Not everyone, however, thought that Joe would make a great **pro**. Some people worried that Joe got injured too much. In college, he often got hurt.

Others worried about his lack of size and strength. National Football League (NFL) teams usually liked bigger, taller quarterbacks with stronger throwing arms.

One person who wasn't worried was Bill Walsh. He was the coach and the **general manager** of the San Francisco 49ers. He felt that Joe was going to be a really special player. In 1979, he picked Joe to be on his team.

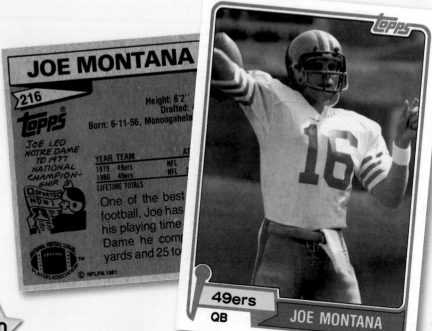

One of Joe's early football cards

Coach Bill Walsh (left) talks to Joe (right) on the sidelines during a game.

Three other quarterbacks were picked ahead of Joe in the 1979 NFL **draft**.

San Francisco Success

Picking Joe for the team was the smartest move Bill Walsh ever made. Joe's passing was a perfect match for his coach's **offensive strategies**.

Just as important, Joe became the team's leader. Other players respected him on and off the field. In the **huddle**, Joe never panicked. He always stayed cool, even when San Francisco fell behind.

However, that didn't happen often. With Joe as quarterback, the 49ers were the NFL's winningest team.

Joe (#16) in a huddle with his team.

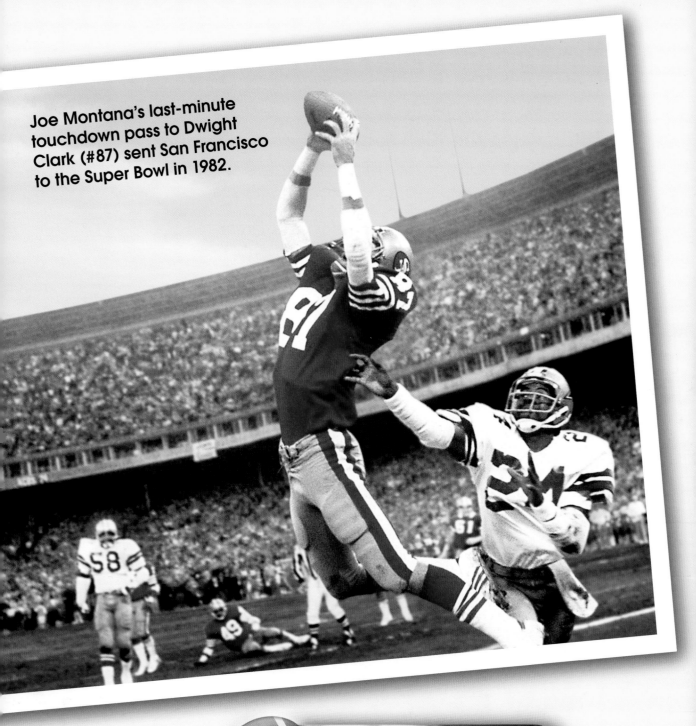

Joe Montana's last-minute touchdown pass to Dwight Clark (#87) sent San Francisco to the Super Bowl in 1982.

Before Super Bowl XXIV (24), Joe had been named Most Valuable Player (MVP) in two of the 49ers' three Super Bowl victories.

Better than Ever

Still, when the 1989 season began, success was not a sure thing. At age 33, Joe was the team's oldest player. Over ten seasons, he'd battled injuries to his back, ribs, and elbows. Could the banged-up quarterback still do the job?

Joe proved that he could—better than ever. In fact, that season he turned in the finest passing performance in NFL history. Joe threw for over 3,500 yards (3,200 m) and 26 touchdowns. The 49ers finished with the best record in the NFL. They were on their way to the playoffs once again.

Joe often took a beating while playing quarterback. After getting hurt during a game against the New England Patriots in 1989, he was taken off the field on a stretcher.

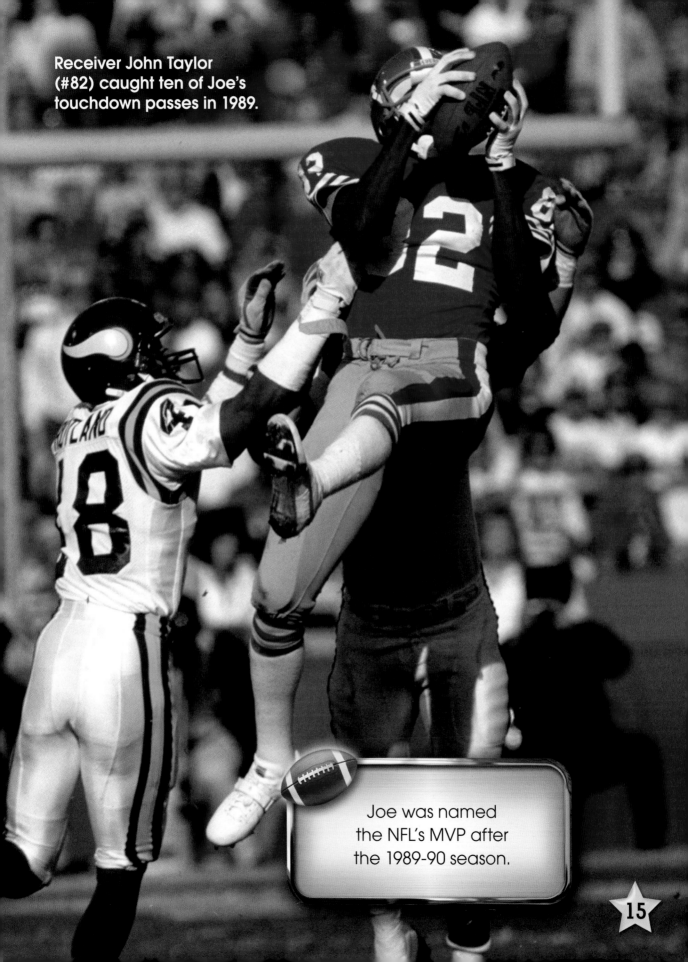

Receiver John Taylor (#82) caught ten of Joe's touchdown passes in 1989.

Joe was named the NFL's MVP after the 1989-90 season.

The Broncos

In the playoffs, Joe helped San Francisco to big wins over the Minnesota Vikings and the Los Angeles Rams. Now they would face the Denver Broncos in Super Bowl XXIV (24).

Denver's quarterback, John Elway, had a more powerful arm than Joe. He was also a talented **rusher**. At any time, he could scramble away and rush up the field like a bull.

In addition, the Broncos had a group of tough defenders. Joe would face waves of tacklers after each and every **snap**.

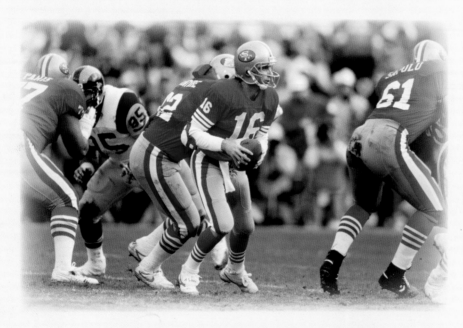

Joe (#16) connected on 26 out of 30 passes in the win against the Rams.

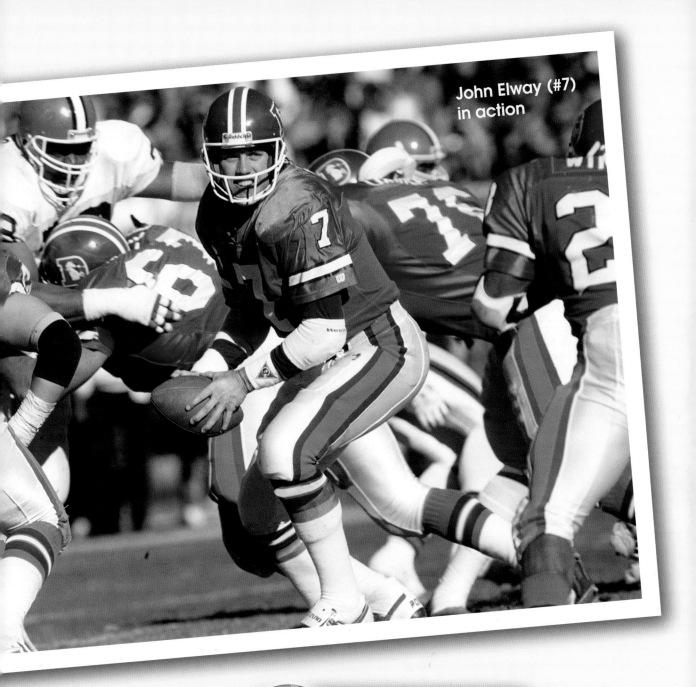

John Elway (#7) in action

During Joe's 11 seasons, the 49ers had beaten every NFL team except one—the Broncos. Denver had won each time the two teams played each other.

Game Time

In a **duel** of top quarterbacks, Joe came out on top from the start. Elway—pressured by San Francisco defenders—kept missing his receivers. Pass after pass fell short or wide.

Joe, on the other hand, was perfect. He threw short passes, medium passes, and long ones. Each throw seemed to hit its target. At one point, Joe completed 13 passes in a row, breaking a Super Bowl record. San Francisco jumped to a 27-3 lead at halftime.

San Francisco defender Daniel Stubbs (#96) celebrates after sacking John Elway (#7).

Joe (#16) high-fives teammate Guy McIntyre during the game.

In the first half of the game, the 49ers scored touchdowns four out of the six times they had the ball.

Record Breaker

Joe didn't let up. During the regular season, the Broncos had given up fewer points than any other team. Today, however, they couldn't keep San Francisco out of the **end zone**.

In all, Joe threw five touchdown passes. Three of them were to his favorite receiver, Jerry Rice. The final score was 55-10. It was the biggest **blowout** in Super Bowl history.

Joe Montana had done it again. For the fourth time since Joe joined the team, the San Francisco 49ers were Super Bowl champions.

Jerry Rice (#80) runs down the field with the ball.

After the game, Joe was named the MVP of the Super Bowl. In 2000, he was named to pro football's Hall of Fame.

★ Key Players ★

There were other key players on the San Francisco 49ers who helped win Super Bowl XXIV (24). Here are two of them.

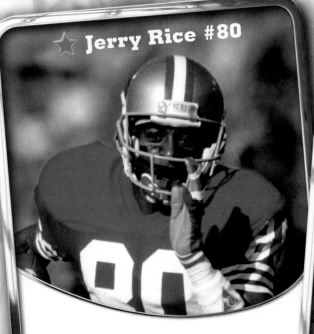

★ Jerry Rice #80

Position: Wide Receiver

Born: 10/13/1962 in Crawford, Mississippi

Height: 6' 2" (1.88 m)

Weight: 200 pounds (91 kg)

Key Plays: Caught three touchdown passes

★ Roger Craig #33

Position: Running Back

Born: 7/10/1960 in Davenport, Iowa

Height: 6' 0" (1.83 m)

Weight: 222 pounds (101 kg)

Key Plays: Rushed for 69 yards (63 m) and one touchdown

★ Glossary ★

All-American
(AWL-uh-MER-uh-kuhn)
a high school or college player
who is named one of the best at
his position in the entire country

blowout (BLOH-out)
a game in which one team wins
easily by scoring many more
points than the other team

Cotton Bowl (KOT-uhn BOHL)
a yearly postseason football
game held in Dallas, Texas,
between two top college teams

defenders (di-FEND-urz)
players who have the job of
trying to stop the other team from
scoring

draft (DRAFT)
an event in which NFL teams
choose college players to be on
their teams

duel (DOO-uhl)
a matchup or contest between
two players on opposing teams

end zone (END ZOHN)
the area at either end of a
football field where touchdowns
are scored

general manager
(JEN-ur-uhl MAN-uh-jur)
the person who chooses the
players for a team

huddle (HUHD-uhl)
a gathering of football players
around a quarterback to talk
about the next play

offensive strategies
(AW-fen-siv STRAT-uh-jeez)
the plans and plays used by a
team to try to score points

pocket (POK-it)
the area where a quarterback
drops back to throw the ball

pro (PROH)
a professional athlete; a person
who is paid to play a sport

receivers (ri-SEE-vurz)
players whose job it is to catch
passes

rusher (RUHSH-ur)
a player whose job it is to run
with the football

snap (SNAP)
when the person playing center
gives the ball to the quarterback
to begin a play

spirals (SPYE-ruhlz)
balls thrown with a tight
spinning motion that makes
them travel farther

Bibliography

Muchnick, Irvin. "Joe Montana: State of the Art." *The New York Times* (December 17, 1989).

Zimmerman, Paul. "Born to Be a Quarterback." *Sports Illustrated* (August 6, 1990).

The San Francisco Chronicle

Read More

Bell, Lonnie. *The History of the San Francisco 49ers.* Mankato, MN: Creative Education (2005).

Stewart, Mark. *The San Francisco (49ers Team Spirit).* Chicago: Norwood House Press (2007).

Learn More Online

To learn more about Joe Montana,
the San Francisco 49ers, and the Super Bowl, visit
www.bearportpublishing.com/SuperBowlSuperstars

Index

1